Samir Saif

Growth Marketing Hack

Tools, skills and the most important strategies.

First published by Samir Saif 2023

Copyright © 2023 by Samir Saif

All rights reserved. No part of this publication may be reproduced, stored or transmitted in any form or by any means, electronic, mechanical, photocopying, recording, scanning, or otherwise without written permission from the publisher. It is illegal to copy this book, post it to a website, or distribute it by any other means without permission.

First edition

ISBN: 9798371475275

This book was professionally typeset on Reedsy
Find out more at reedsy.com

Contents

1. Introduction and definition of the most important terms 1
Introduction and definition of the most important terms 1
What does 1
What is the most important thing in growth marketing? 1
The scientific methodology it employs growth marketing. 1
Key aspects of growth marketing 1
Idea generation 1
Goals, K Pis, and metrics. Why is this important? 1
What is North Star metric? 1
OMTM (One Metric That Matters) 1
ISM vs OMIT: Why they need to co-exist? 1
2. Growth marketing skills you need & why they matter? 12
Growth marketing skills you need & why they matter? 12
1. Data analytics 12
2. Optimization 12
3. People skills 12
4. Marketing 12
5. Basic design 12
6. Experimentation 12
7. Analytical thinking 12
8. Problem-Solving Skills 12
9. Analytical and critical thinking 12
10. Active Listening Skills 12
3. Growth Marketing Tools 20

1. Growth Hacking Canvas: A Glance At The Tools To Generate Growth Ideas..20
2. Cyfe Software 20
3. GoodData Platform 20
4. Sisense Platform 20
5. Tableau Platform 20
6. Grow.com BI tool 20
7. Marketo marketing software 20
9. Keap complete sales, marketing 20
10. Sharp Spring service marketing tool 20
11. Active Demand Marketing Software. 20
4. Growth Hacking Strategies. Tips to Get More Traffic 29
Grow through emails 29
YouTube growth strategy 29
Hub Spot growth strategy 29
5. The most important questions and inquiries 37
What is the right growth equation for your company? 37
What do you think might improve the effectiveness of those two Teams' collaboration in a marketing-led company? 37
What would be the the building blocks that you start with? 37
What are the favorite tools for gathering customer and market data? 37
What distinguishes growth marketing from growth hacking?..........37
How do you sell this growth mindset to a development team? 37
How would you assist a business that has a B2C product but is unsure of its target market? 37
Afterword..51

1.

1.
    2.
    3.
    4.
5.
    6.
    7.
    8.
    9.
    10.

2.
    1.
    2.
    3.
    4.
    5.
    6.
    7.
    8.
    9.
    10.
    11.

3.
    1.

    2.
    3.
    4.
    5.
    6.
    7.
    8.
    9.
    10.
4.
    1.
    2.
    3.
5.
    1.
    2.
    3.
    4.
    5.
    6.
    7.

1

Introduction and definition of the most important terms

Introduction and definition of the most important terms

Today, we'll talk about growth marketing. Therefore, I want to define growth marketing. We'll go into further detail about the goals, K Pis, and measurements.

You need growth marketing strategies, tools, and abilities. Tips to Increase Traffic, queries and questions, and their connections among themselves.

Therefore, you should now be familiar with the fundamentals of growth marketing, the frameworks and tools available to you, how to create growth goals which is crucial measure them, as well as how to use the Growth Canvas tool and the idealization and experimentation process.

We sincerely hope that you will take care of everything. I'd like to get a sense of where you stand right now in terms of your understanding of growth marketing.

What does "growth marketing" refers to?

Growth marketing is really the data-driven process of rapid experimentation, along the whole funnel with your product, and across all channels to identify the most efficient ways to grow.

There are many different explanations for growth marketing and growth hacking out there This is an explanation that we really like. So we are trying to hold onto that.

In growth marketing, experimentation is prioritized over task-based thinking. Usually, it has to do with the data-driven component.

Of course, thinking through the entire funnel is also a crucial component. However, I'll get to that shortly. I'll delve a little bit more deeply into each of these areas.

In order to find out what works best, especially for startups or businesses who are trying something new, we want to test a lot of things, or as we like to say, everything.

What is the most important thing in growth marketing?

Growth marketing's most crucial component and the one that sets it apart from all other marketing approaches is testing.

The tried-and-true strategy for growth marketing success involves ongoing, rigorous testing of internet marketing initiatives and campaigns.

To learn quickly and avoid wasting money on things that might not work for you, it is really crucial to include a lot of tests into your schedule.

Small details, such as distinct call to actions, button colors, or the amount of text you use in your email or on social media, are therefore important.

Any channels, such as, say, Linked In, Facebook advertisements, Instagram, or even offline. So anything you can think of is something that can be tested and having this mindset will also actually assist you to make decisions faster.

Because it's extremely simple to simply have this mindset of "let's just test it, in an MVP version, a tiny version, see if it works or not, and then take it from there" if you sit in a meeting and attempt to decide whether or not you should go for something. As a result, we attempt to constantly remind ourselves to test, test, test every day.

The scientific methodology it employs growth marketing.

Another way to consider growth marketing is essentially to consider the scientific methodology it employs. So, as I said before, we don't merely perform tasks; rather, we conduct experiments, which essentially entails developing a hypothesis.

As a result, you make an assumption, then a hypothesis, and finally a test scenario. The structure, or guidelines, as it were, for actually carrying out that, is effectively what the test scenario is.

Then you examine the data you have collected, conduct an analysis of it, and decide whether to accept or reject the hypothesis. Based on your decision, you can then revise your original hypothesis.

So it's this circle that always goes around, and you don't really stop until you find the sweet spot. Even if you find the sweet spot, you still try to learn from it, and make it even better.

It's really between these three different areas. So it's between creative marketing, experiments and data, and automation and engineering.

Growth marketing comes together at this point. Due to the fact that you can sometimes focus entirely on the creative aspects of your work and other times you have to put on your analytical hat and look at the facts, this job is also incredibly enjoyable.

Finally, you can experiment a lot with engineering and automation, either on your own or with help from others. It's basically a blend of these three things.

This is really when growth hacking can happen, when these three things come together. You don't have to cover every aspect perfectly, but this should give you an idea.

Key aspects of growth marketing

Marketing is basically the culmination of all marketing activities. But putting it all together and being aware of the resources available are key.

So this really helps in the idealization stage when you start to kind of look beyond, say, simply performance marketing or social media, and you think along all these other lines, and then construct your hypothesis and start experimenting.

Now, how does the procedure itself operate? What steps do you take to set up these experiments?

Idea generation

For everyone involved in marketing, the first step is to generate ideas. It's a very undervalued phase since after working for a firm or your own business for some time, you may forget to set aside the time necessary to truly produce new ideas.

As a result, we constantly strive to reach that point, take a seat, and consider what else an individual or the team could do. Once you have a long list of ideas in place, then you organize and prioritize them. 'Cause obviously, you can't do everything at once, and there's different methods for that as well, and then you start testing.

Once you have the tests in place, and they're up and running for a while, you then analyze them, and then the fun starts with optimizing, where you really see what works well, what doesn't work so well.

You find bottlenecks, and then you try to experiment even more, and try to improve those areas, and then you basically repeat. So again, here, it's a process, it's a circle, and growth hacking basically works in that way, that you don't just generate ideas once.

Then you just kind of keep doing whatever you've been doing, but you force yourself to keep going back to generating ideas, to then learn and see what works and what doesn't work. I briefly mentioned the funnel before.

So, the idea is to really think along this whole funnel, and that's also one way of differentiating it to traditional marketing, where your focus is usually on awareness and acquisition.

In growth marketing, it's really also about thinking of how to activate users, how to make sure that they come back. So retention. How can we make most of them and maybe turn them into our ambassadors? And that's referral.

Finally, how can you experiment with income as a topic and as a marketer to discover how you might generate more of it, of course?

So, the goal here is not just to increase sales, although that is the end goal, but also to experiment with how you present prices on your website, for instance, by offering different bundles and discounts.

Even as a marketer, you may consider all of that and attempt to experiment along the lines of, well, the complete AAARRR funnel. As a result, it's also known as the pirate funnel or the AAARRR funnel. Dave McClure essentially thought of it.

It's a really beneficial tool for us to look along the entire funnel when dealing with our customers rather than simply getting stuck in, say, acquisition, which is always the most obvious decision to make. I'm good. What a succinct introduction to growth marketing that was.

Goals, KPIs, and metrics. Why is this important?

Because, growth marketers work data-driven, so of course, you need to have some goals, some measurable outcome, to put some numbers to what you're working towards.

You need to put some numbers to your growth. That's why this is especially important, and here, this little saying, we really always like to kick this section off with the sentence, if it's not worth measuring, it's not worth doing.

> If it's not worth measuring, it's not worth doing.

This may seem so simple at first, but many startups, businesses, and other entities get into the trap of focusing on figures that, particularly in the beginning, may make them feel good or appear good to them but may not actually be that significant for what we want to accomplish. As opposed to actionable metrics that we do want to focus on, these metrics are what we like to refer to as vanity metrics.

Therefore, a vanity metric might be, for instance, if you're a company in whatever area, but you have some sort of social media accounts and a following there, and you want to concentrate on collecting 10K followers on either Facebook or Instagram, and that is your aim.

Even if it could make you feel good and look nice, it's unlikely that this would ultimately increase your income. This is a "vanity metric," then.

This is why, in growth marketing, there's those two kind of metrics that we have defined, that we should focus on. On the one hand, it's the OMIT. That's short for one metric that matters. Versus the North Star metric. What either of those mean, let's start with the North Star metric.

What is North Star metric?

It is the company goal. It is really what the whole company wants to achieve, wants to work towards.

So it's kind of set in stone, unless you decide at one point, you want to change your whole business model, or parts of it, of course, then it can happen that you will change your North Star metric, but usually it is set.

It is based on your business model. It is based on what your service offering, or your product offering will be. So this is also where it can only be one North Star metric, and it must be broad enough so the whole organization can contribute.

So it's not just through marketing activities, but ideally, the whole organization can contribute, and it ideally, is also something that will help you generate revenue, or even profit.

OMTM (One Metric That Matters)

OMIT stands for one metric that matters and this is not opposed to the North Star metric, but it very much ties into what the North Star metric tries to achieve. As a growth hacker, your sole emphasis in your everyday job will be the OMIT, or the one metric that matters.

The OMIT, however, does, will, and should vary, in contrast to the North Star metric. Say that we devote the following two, four, or five weeks to working on this OMIT.

This is unimportant. But it is adaptable and will change dependent on where you are in the marketing funnel, on your trip, and on your growth journey.

ISM vs OMIT: Why they need to co-exist?

The North Star metric basically is the roof of all the other goals, and the Om's very much tied into what we're trying to achieve with the North Star metric.

The example north start metric revenue is provided here. Of sure, I would agree it is legitimate. This North Star metric is reliable. However, being a little more specific would make sense.

I therefore frequently utilize well-known instances, like Airborne. Naturally, Airborne wants to make money. However, I believe their North Star metric would be something like nights booked on the platform, and this, of course, ties into revenue.

They want to achieve profit, or probably already are. Just to give you a sense of what the North Star meter would be, listen to something similar on Spottily for, I believe, minutes.

As for the Oms, as I previously stated, they change, they should change, and they will change, and this is essentially your daily focus as a growth hacker.

As examples, I'd like to work on retention right away. In the following week, month, or whenever, we might work on raising the average cart size, and so on and so forth. I believe you understand.

***

2

Growth marketing skills you need & why they matter?

Growth marketing skills you need & why they matter?

We are frequently asked what abilities growth marketers require, or what growth marketing entails. There are many different topics that we attempt to address. Obviously, you cannot be an authority in each of these fields. However, the objective is also for us to know what is available to us when working with startups, for instance, and then to sort of come up with ideas or trials in various areas of these things. Even if you aren't able to cover everything, you might have some team members who are skilled in, say, SEO.

You could try pairing them up with a programmer and have them sort of work as a team. In essence, what we're trying to express is that we don't just concentrate on one aspect of marketing growth. In order to contribute to the cycle of development and growth, growth marketers must be adaptable. Although we can't go through every skill a growth marketer will require, we do want to focus on the most crucial ones and explain why they are so crucial.

1. Data analytics

Growth marketers need to be able to comprehend data and use it to inform strategic decisions. This ability is essential for growth marketers to avoid squandering time and resources on ineffective marketing plans. You may determine precisely which elements of your existing customer journey are well-liked by customers by using analytics to evaluate retention, engagement, activation, and more.

You can identify your highest-value customers and learn what keeps them retained long-term. You can then use these insights to craft personalized campaigns and experiences that drive desired behaviors for certain cohorts. Amplitude's suite of products gives growth marketers invaluable insight concerning customer engagement patterns and key metrics.

2. Optimization

Growth marketers must be able to handle search engine optimization (SEO), conversion rate optimization (CRO), and marketing campaign optimization. These key facets of growth marketing carry customer engagement past the point of acquisition. SEO skills will increase customer awareness and acquisition, boosting your conversion rates before you even optimize them.

When your optimization skills as a growth marketer are top-tier, you'll be able to take pride in a marketing map that guides customers to greater satisfaction and better lifetime value. Your marketing campaign optimization will also contribute to better customer engagement. And, of course, your CRO abilities will increase the likelihood of those customers sticking around.

3. People skills

To succeed in their position, growth marketers need to have good interpersonal skills. Understanding the needs and desires of the customer is a key component of growth marketing. How could someone create a marketing strategy that would be successful for a target market they don't truly understand?

Data analysis, in the opinion of some, can close this gap. You must be able to put yourself in the user's position if you want to be a growth marketer. Continually honing your interpersonal skills will help you increase client acquisition and retention. You can't rely entirely on facts and ignore your soft skills since human connection is far too nuanced.

4. Marketing

You will obviously require a broad understanding of marketing if you want to succeed as a growth marketer. Getting more people to notice and remember your business is at the heart of marketing.

Additionally, it's critical to focus on a few specific areas because doing so will give your work a human touch.

A growth marketer must be able to coordinate powerful marketing campaigns with both the big picture and unique rationalization tactics in mind. Maybe you're especially good at relating to people through social media or handling customers' concerns. Lean into your strengths and people will remember your brand.

5. Basic design

As a GM, you'll benefit greatly from a basic understanding of web graphics and design. Accessibility features such as text size, contrast, and loading speed are also crucial.

For optimal company growth, your marketing campaigns and web pages must look appealing and be highly accessible. A growth marketer must be comfortable with basic user interface (UI) and user experience (UX) design.

You'll also need to test things quickly to make sure that any changes you make have had the desired effect. The more efficient you are throughout the testing process, the faster the company's product will be able to grow.

6. Experimentation

Growth marketers who truly excel in their roles are creative disruptors who confront the status quo with challenging ideas and innovative solutions. Trial and error are essential parts of the process, and you may need to conduct A/B testing or use behavioral analytics to gauge the success of your new methods.

Experimentation is key in a growth marketer's creative process since you need to acquire data-based knowledge of how to allocate your resources. Housecall Pro used Amplitude Experiment to laser in on opportunities for improvement within their web optimization strategies.

7. Analytical thinking

Analytical thinking is essential for success because data and plans are such fundamental components of a growth marketer's job. To accomplish company goals effectively, you'll need to have a strong ability to prioritize projects. You'll also need to be methodical in your approach.

Unclear instructions or muddled information have no place in growth marketing. A top-notch growth marketer must sift through massive datasets for the most crucial trends before distilling them into clear, actionable insights. To make sure that each target is successful, you'll need to use analytical thinking together with excellent communication to share your findings with others.

Growth marketers need a strong ability to analyze new ideas and either validate them quickly or provide efficient and constructive feedback for improvement. A background in skillfully organized data interpretation will help you here as will the ability to prioritize which areas of the marketing strategy need the most immediate attention.

8. Problem-Solving Skills

Regardless of the type of job you have or the career you want to follow, being able to solve problems well will help you succeed and make an impression. Rial Farrell, author of The Manager's Dilemma, claims that "a person who solves issues and makes decisions is perceived as someone who can get things done."

To reach the finish line, there are a number of stages you must do. Your career will require these talents more and more as you advance. You become more useful to any firm as you develop your problem-solving abilities.

If you don't know what the issue is, you can't solve it. When a problem is identified, you must assess its potential consequences. "A important skill here is being able to analyze the size, impact, and costs [of a problem]".

9. Analytical and critical thinking

Develop your analytical and critical thinking skills so you can review the impact of your work and adjust it accordingly.

Honing this skill can also be helpful when it comes to trends and whether your company should participate in them. What this looks like: Comparing social media metrics month by month to determine what type of post does best.

10. Active Listening Skills

The technique of actively listening allows one to obtain knowledge from another person or group. It entails listening carefully, refraining from interruptions, and taking the time to comprehend what the speaker is saying.

The "active" component entails taking action to elicit information that might not otherwise be disclosed. By actively listening, you shift your attention from your own needs to those of your interviewer or potential employer.

Using this method can help you feel less anxious during an interview. It's crucial to avoid interjecting or, worse, attempting to respond to the interviewer's question before you understand what they are asking.

Developing rapport and trust are two active listening strategies. Consider the circumstances that can arise during an interview and devise plans that will enable you to listen attentively.

* * *

3

Growth Marketing Tools

A digital marketing dashboard collects data from several sources, such as social media, digital advertising, email campaigns, and website analytics, and shows it all in one place in real-time. Some software programs are made particularly to function as stand-alone business intelligence dashboards.

They give a quick rundown of how marketing campaigns are doing. Some marketing automation solutions include built-in reporting features, allowing marketing data to be input and examined on the same platform.

- Linked In Business Manager is basically where you would be setting up all your Linked In ads, if you were to run any.
- Google Analytics is where you get analytical, where you analyze your data of all your different marketing efforts.
- SEMrush is a tool that will audit your website.
- Facebook Business Manager is the same what is Linked In Business Manager for Linked In. This is where you would run your Google campaigns, search campaigns, and so forth.

- Canva is a free graphic design tool that lets you design maybe ads, or also something for social media posts without much of a graphic design knowledge.
- The research, however, would only be applicable to that marketing data and couldn't be modified to look at data from other programs like CRMs or social media management systems.

Now that we understand the basics of what marketing dashboards are, lets take a look at 11 of the top options available today.

1. Growth Hacking Canvas: A Glance At The Tools To Generate Growth Ideas.

The Growth Canvas is a tool to help you visualize your marketing efforts. It allows you to really have everything together in one place. It's also quite fun at that, because it is usually an activity you do together with your team. It involves quite a lot of brainstorming, so it can always be a fun team activity together.

Let's start top left, the SMART goals. SMART goals, they're S-M-A-R-T goals, because they're abbreviations. It basically means your goals need to be specific, they need to be measurable, as we said before, attainable, relevant and timely.

This example here, increase new users by 20% next month. They fulfilled all the criteria because it's specific, I would say. It's measurable because we put the amount that we want to achieve.

It is attainable, of course, here, it's a little bit out of context, but usually, within the context you know if it's achievable within the next month or not. It is relevant, also within context, you will know whether it's relevant or not, and it is timely, because it says next month. We kind of need to have some sort of a timeframe, time period, deadline when we want to achieve this goal.

So, the target audience might also be very straightforward, because of course, if you run a business, work for a business, you will already have figured out which audience to target.

Also here, this is maybe not really part of the Growth Canvas, but always take your time to really study your personas, create your personas, and the outcomes of this, also a nice team activity.

The outcomes of this, you can put here in the target audience, so you have it all in one picture together. Budget, yes. I think this one is really self-explanatory. Because what amount of your funds that you have will you allocate to marketing actions?

you can also of course be a bit more specific. Maybe your overall budget, but also which project, when you have budget, will you allocate on which action, on which area? Yes, and growth areas, this is where you can kind of pin down what you want to focus on.

So what I was saying is, here, it also gets to brainstorming, based on the goal to define before, based on the growth areas you decided to focus on, and also of course, based.

2. Cyfe Software

Cyfe is a web-based, standalone business dashboard that brings together data from marketing channels, web analytics, finance, sales, social media, and more. It includes pre-built dashboard templates to make it easier to get started.

Although there is a free plan for one person and up to two dashboards, organizations can select from four premium plans or an agency plan that is more appropriate for their requirements.

Additionally, Cyfe has access to a wide range of services, such as social media networks and statistics on keyword rankings.

3. GoodData Platform

GoodData is a stand-alone, cloud-based BI platform that focuses on aiding marketers in comprehending the wants and behaviors of their customers.

Interactive dashboards are used to obtain tactical insights for particular campaigns and programs as well as to assist decision-makers in understanding the overall impact of marketing on the organization.

Custom attribution models, channel ROI analytics, and conversion funnel tracking are all features of GoodData's marketing analytics solution.

4. Sisense Platform

A standalone business analytics dashboard called Sisense was created to aid non-IT professionals in comprehending and visualizing their data.

Through integrated connectors, a drag-and-drop user interface, and custom filters, it gathers and arranges data from various sources. Geographical maps, KPI gauges, line charts, scatter plots, and pie charts are examples of visualization characteristics.

With Excel as well as well-known marketing applications like Salesforce, Adwords, and Google Analytics, built-in connectors enable plug-and-play interoperability. Additionally, it provides a particular setup for analytics on lead creation.

5. Tableau Platform

Due to its innovation and reliable platform, Tableau is a leader in the business intelligence space as a standalone data visualization solution. Depending on the level of access each employee need, businesses can choose from a variety of licenses for their team.

Tableau has numerous connectors with services like GitHub and. CSV files to Spotify and Fitbit. If your data connection does not already exist, you can create it yourself thanks to the open-source guidelines provided by the connections community to integrate as many data sources into Tableau as possible (or with the help of a developer).

6. Grow.com BI tool

Grow.com is a stand-alone business intelligence (BI) application that provides marketers with access to a robust dashboard and business intelligence reports with real-time data.

Grow.com will automatically pull data into dashboards for the most recent reports by integrating the technologies in your marketing stack.

Customized branded reports enable agencies to create client-specific reports for dissemination and C-levels to compile information from several campaigns.

Because no coding is required, adoption is quicker, and anybody can learn to analyze data thanks to the platform's design, which makes data analytics available throughout an organization.

7. Marketo marketing software

With over 3,000 clients and an estimated 21% market share, Marketo is one of the largest B2B marketing software providers.

Their platform includes a ton of pre-built dashboards and tailored reports for reviewing cross-channel campaign income, benchmarking your performance against rivals, tracking the lead funnel, assessing email campaigns, and more.

Dashboards are presented under the "oeAnalytics" tab in the online application and can be adjusted based on user role.

9. Keap complete sales, marketing

Keap, formerly known as Infusionsoft, is a complete sales, marketing, and eCommerce solution designed for businesses of any size.

The MA side of their platform provides dashboard analytics through its reports tab, including web, social, and email stats, campaign visualization, and lead tracking.

Although Keaps analytics are less sophisticated than other solutions, it still provides good overall value, considering a single subscription price covers automation, CRM, e Commerce, and basic BI.

10. Sharp Spring service marketing tool

Sharp Spring is a full-service marketing instrument for organizations and agencies that aims to nurture more leads and boost sales.

The program integrates sales and marketing automation to assist businesses in creating campaigns, pipelines, and automated workflows that increase sales.

The marketing tools for driving growth include sophisticated email, online lead, and campaign tracking systems with strong web analytics and reporting.

Companies can analyze exactly how their efforts are performing and where efficiencies may be made thanks to analytics and reports that are ROI-driven.

11. Active Demand Marketing Software.

Marketing software for freelancers and businesses is called Active Demand. The solution was created with agencies in mind and can control numerous marketing initiatives from a single interface.

Nearly all of your agency's marketing activities, including call monitoring, appointment scheduling, event marketing, and website multivariate testing, are covered by the automation tools.

The reporting option combines drag and drop marketing reports with visually appealing scheduled reports, alerts and notifications, and branded reporting.

* * *

4

Growth Hacking Strategies. Tips to Get More Traffic

Before we begin, I want to share with you a very important quote from a man by the name of Adam Nash, who says that all good companies take growth seriously because without it, you won't be able to increase your revenue, traffic, or sales.

For instance, if you are familiar with Facebook, you know that their internal metric when they first started out was how many more users were they adding per day and that they weren't just looking at it as a pure number.

You can't only focus on the most popular channels when you're attempting to expand since those channels fill up quickly. Therefore, you must be very careful about how you approach your audience.

You must ascertain the exact channels that your customers use. When Dropbox originally launched, it was valued at over $10 billion USD.

What's wrong with that? Well, their product is only $99 a year. Did you know that when they first started out, they actually tried to acquire customers on Google AdWords before they tried doing any growth hacking or anything else?

Just because a consumer pays them $99 doesn't mean they make $99 from that sale; there are costs associated with that customer, such as support expenses.

Shopify has over 30,000 plus businesses paying for Shopify Salesforce has over a hundred thousand. 37signals has over 150 Yammer has over 200 thousand Constant Contact has over 400 thousand.

MailChimp has over 2 million Google Apps over 4 million fresh books 4.5 google analytics over 30 million businesses are using Google Analytics. Evernote has a lot of users. so how do you actually do these integrations. These integrations have to make your product better and the other person's product better. Evernote is a place where you just take notes what do you think yes or no no it's ok.

Integration with Google Analytics makes sense for the reason that if they are already using it, we can say, "Hey, Google Analytics will show you or shows you what OK, me your website or and KISSmetrics tells you what happened right in which we can actually give them more data on top of Google Analytics that benefits them and it benefits us."

Ask your customers what other services what other products what other tools do you use what other websites do you go on.

This will help you identify what solutions you should potentially integrate with. It has to be a win-win once you do that you need to make your partner pages awesome. The more integrations companies have, the longer they'll end up sticking around and paying them.

"Once you start getting attraction 3 you need a head up the companies are integrating with and try to get them to promote this integration to their user base and you'll be shocked they actually want to promote it why".

Grow through emails

Everyone has an email account well there's a gmail or hotmail or at Microsoft you know your company that you work for or whatever it may be. If you can figure out how to tap it you can actually get a big customer base quickly.

This is how people like Facebook and Twitter growth even currently LinkedIn example write a lot of them all grow through emails. We'll give you additional free space if you enter the emails of more of your coworkers, incentivizing them to invite their friends.

Facebook is aware that you only need 10 or 30 friends within the first seven days, and that number may even be as high as 30. They know that if you have 10 or 30 friends within that time frame, you're very likely to continue using Facebook indefinitely.

Good onboarding, for instance, would be when you sign up for Facebook and say, "All right cool now that you've signed up let's connect you with your friends put in your email so we can see which of your friends are already on Facebook if none of them are it's like all right."

If the onboarding isn't good, their friends won't actually use the product. Once you've invited your friends to Facebook, they'll tell you to create your profile, add an image, your bio, your birthdate, and other information. The cool thing about email addresses is that you don't even need to ask people for their name and email.

When you're doing this process; just tell them to sign up through Twitter or Facebook and when they click a button, your conversion rate will increase by a whopping 30+%, which is enormous, and you can quickly access all of their contacts and other information.

Dropbox is a great example of this right in which they try to get you to invite more people more people you invite more storage you get that's why they you total is it you got to measure the number of people in every company or every person has in their contact list this will help you determine what the potential you can actually go for.

YouTube growth strategy

When I started out I wanted people to embed my company's product on their website. I was like yeah show your data to the world show them you know how much traffic you're getting.

There was no good reason on why they should embed it I just wanted to do it. People embed YouTube videos because they want to share something.

You have to give people a reason why they're gonna embed you can't expect someone to bed something on their website for no reason. If you can figure out what these actions are you'll get more people to stick around for a lot longer.

You also want to make it easy as possible to embed make them quick uh you know box it automatically highlights it all they click a copy link and they can embed it on to their site right copy paste.

You can even create little widgets like hey have a wordpress site click here to get the WordPress version have tumblr click hereto get the tumblr version those are all examples.

When doing these embeds, many people say, "Oh, we kept the back-links. Do you know why back-links are valuable? It's so we can get more search engine traffic and higher search engine ranks." You should optimize for search, but don't worry over it.

Additionally testing pertinent call to actions, they discovered that displaying pertinent movies worked best. Make the call to action and links relevant rather than being overly greedy to prevent influencing the search results.

Your search traffic will eventually rise if you employ pertinent anchor text rather than anchor text that is keyword-rich. Powered by badges are probably commonplace by now.

But the thing with powered by widgets is that people frequently click through to them, and some of them even result in sign-ups. So, okay, swish with these powered by badges; people need to know what you're powering.

Hub Spot growth strategy

Hub Spot offers a free grater that tells you what you're doing wrong with your marketing, and they recently went public; they're valued at almost a billion dollars.

They'll say things like, "Hey, you're doing this, isn't this wrong, and by the way, sign up for hot sauce." highly efficient A nice example of a good free tool is HubSpot. How quickly is your app in comparison to others?

This is yet another new Relic measurement. When you're doing this free stuff, you need to map it out to the customer decision-making. Kitt's ebooks and PDFs are all excellent examples of free stuff that you could end up using.

It's not always necessary to start from scratch and invest a lot of time and money in development. If you can test an existing product, reuse it, and launch it, do it right the first time. If it succeeds, you can modify it and then spend money on it.

Ebooks and instructions for using things are the best freebies available. Free items can be converted into revenue, for instance. Dropbox, which offers free storage and earns a ton of money by writing a ton of stuff for free, has had great success. Inform your business contacts about your goods and services.

Growth hacking isn't just about getting more users; it's also about giving your customers greater value and benefits. You also have no excuse not to produce money; just because firms like Snapchat and Pinterest are valued at billions of dollars without generating any revenue, it doesn't follow that you can do the same.

* * *

5

The most important questions and inquiries

What is the right growth equation for your company?

Every person we talk to has a different perspective on marketing-led growth, so I think it would be good for our listeners to know where you stand on the subject. All businesses can benefit from increased revenue, product leads, and marketing leads. how you perceive those tactics to be.

Marketing requires a mindset of thinking about pipeline thinking about actual opportunities as opposed to just lead generation. I think marketing when you look at the marketing side it's when you've actually you've created an engine that is providing enough pipeline to feed and grow the organization.

While marketing is extremely essential to us, a large portion of our business still comes from the networks of contacts that our sales representatives have built up over the course of many years in the local area.

The business can begin to rely on that marketing engine more once you get it up and running and it starts to expand and flourish beautifully. In the modern world, I've observed some conflict between the sales and marketing teams over who is in charge of what, and there are several discussions taking on about how those two teams can cooperate.

What do you think might improve the effectiveness of those two Teams' collaboration in a marketing-led company?

Look, where marketing and sales converge can either be a place of intense conflict and toxicity or a peaceful path to success. If you want the latter, you need strong sales and marketing leaders who comprehend one another and see each other as partners rather than in conflictual Us and Them scenarios.

Usually, this problem can be resolved by changing how each person approaches marketing. Leaders of each department need to work in lockstep to achieve a harmonious relationship. Sales should take some ownership of their own success and give plenty of feedback to marketing on what works and what doesn't.

A lot of what they do is going to help marketing get better which doesn't always happen" If that is harmonious it's going to be great if it's combative it's Going to be effective.

If you were the CMO of an early stage software company what would you start looking at to build your initial marketing growth plan.

What would be the the building blocks that you start with?

In general, the smaller the company, the more money it should spend on sales and marketing. For example, if a company has revenues between $10 million and $15 million, it should probably spend more than 20% of those revenues on marketing.

You probably won't have all the necessary expertise and resources in-house, such as knowledge of SEO, ABM, and a wide range of other strategies, including possibly bdrs.

You must establish proficiency around these things and launch your website and digital strategy. So, until you're mature enough to bring them in-house, you can use agencies for that. There are many sophisticated agencies that you can call upon to go do those things for you.

Your differentiation is crucial, but building a brand takes time. Once your revenue reaches 50 to 150 million, it will be around 11 to 12 before we consider marketing, and once it reaches 200 to 500 million, it will drop to about 6 to 7 before we consider marketing.

You actually notice marketing slowing down as the firm grows, despite marketing expenses growing linearly with company growth. Oh, definitely over a billion dollars in revenue growth, which is typically less than 4%.

Throwing more money at digital, hiring more people, and other strategies won't help until your brand has grown to the point where it can stand on its own two feet, in my opinion. As Word of Mouth gets larger you would expect that the brand is well established and Word of mouth at that stage tip right yeah.

As you reach that sort of mid size it gets closer to 50 50 and as you get bigger you need fewer people and so you need more people and a little less spend. As a company grows, how does the mix of discretionary and headcount change? What about challenges?

If we consider a company that has surpassed the 50 or 100 million dollar revenue mark, I have to assume that even though the marketing budget will be lower, there will still be new challenges and new goals.

I would say that my secret sauce is one of the hardest hurdles I've encountered, but the way I approach every firm I work with is to attempt to get the hardcore lead generating funnel rolling.

I focus everything on short to medium term lead generation. You should try to develop the top of the funnel. There are several simple things you can do to create that early pipe.

You've always got to be ramping up the brand on the longer term top of funnel spend in line with that and getting that balance right is really important.

Growth a longer-term pipeline that is based on brand recognition, customer advocacy, customer success, people recognizing you in the market, and word-of-mouth marketing all requires investment, propagation, and building.

All of that stuff does need to be invested in, propagated, and built; you can't just concentrate on short-term pipe generation.

There are reasons to do that in the beginning in various market conditions and environments, but there is definitely a reason to also look to the future or your pipeline growth will stagnate.

What are the favorite tools for gathering customer and market data?

Let's go into the specifics of how you actually carry out that pipeline construction, website building, and all those other mechanics surrounding inbound marketing, pipeline creation, and even other parts around it.

I always maintain that a data-driven marketing plan is the cornerstone of a successful marketing strategy. Everyone talks about being data-driven, and while I agree with what you said, I do think that marketing is just as much an operations as it is a science.

It used to be all about the arts, but now science has a significant influence, and I think we need to keep in mind that combining the two is what nowadays defines a successful company.

You know, there are some incredibly talented technical people in the marketing world who know a lot more than I do, and you know there are a lot of left-brain or right-brain people, but I think you have to bring that together.

I consider the Salesforce automation system to be the most crucial marketing tool. When salespeople's hygiene is not up to par, it truly irritates me.

A marketing team needs a 100 percent accurate CRM system to be effective. I believe that the value of having an accurate CRM system from a sales standpoint cannot be overstated. We base our business operations on pipeline analysis and predicting sales based on previous sales activity.

As a marketing leader, I spend all of my time analyzing CRM in the manner that you would anticipate a sales leader to do. I base my marketing plans and budgets on what I find there.

Everyone would probably agree that's crucial, especially for marketing as you call out yet it feels like you're depending on a sales order to carry out this technique. You can assume that the sales leader is doing all the necessary steps to spread the hygiene standards that you would like in the CRM.

Do you in marketing have a role in ensuring that the data is accurate, or am I solely dependent on this dear sales staff and let's hope that it is accurate because if it is not, there would be an impact?

If we can't demonstrate that we are getting a return from a particular investment because the attribution is incorrect since sales didn't handle that portion of it correctly, we risk having our budget slashed.

If we don't have reliable data, you must explain to them what this means. I engage directly with sales executives to assist them understand what we're looking at, how it plays back into our investments, and what we're doing to support that team.

This helps them put the proper amount of pressure and onus on their teams to understand the partnership and what it's there for, and it keeps marketing focused on the end result. I mean all these things have an impact on investment decisions and stuff, so it comes back to that relationship.

I've observed that, as you mentioned, the marketing team is very interested in what the sales team is doing and getting insights from that, as well as becoming very plugged into the Salesforce automation tool.

On the other hand, I've also observed sales leaders getting very excited to see what marketing is doing and looking inside the marketing tools that they're using. Sales always wanted to know what marketing was doing. Marketing spends very little time trying to tell sales how to go run a sales process right.

This is more about the two teams coming together to ensure that the data that both organizations input and use is complete and accurate so that they can service and support each other more effectively. If you've got brand equity in it it's something you need to think twice about and not play with" "You never mess with names without thinking through all the consequences".

Your ability to stay relevant and keep creating demand can be massively effective if you were to change your or a company name. When you do go through Acquisitions when you do acquire companies is never to just assume that people in the company you've Acquired and the roles and the titles they have are the same as they are in your company.

Always look at people and individuals and learn what they do and what they're responsible for. It would be beneficial to know that you have this individual in this seat with this title, what their actual responsibilities are, and what degree of talents they possess.

I'm not sure if it is a reasonable demand to make of the company you are acquiring, but it seems like it would be during the process, because many businesses use the same label to signify very different things.

Make sure you're spending in both short-term pipeline generation and long-term brand development. Once your progress plateaus and you don't suddenly develop a brand, it's incredibly difficult to catch up. Since brand creation takes time, you must be extremely diligent in maintaining it.

What distinguishes growth marketing from growth hacking?

marketing for growth and growth hacking The two things are identical. We initially referred to ourselves as "growth hackers," but we soon understood that many businesses don't associate that term with anything positive.

Going in as a growth hacker is quite challenging, especially in the corporate sector. As was already said, a synonym for growth marketing is. So it's basically the same thing; growth is the key. You may either hack it or sell it.

How do you sell this growth mindset to a development team?

When we deal with our clients, we truly persuade them to take a comprehensive approach rather than just concentrating on marketing or product development, and when you look at your growth canvas, you might already be able to integrate other teams. The marketing staff does not necessarily have to be involved.

Everyone in the organization needs to adopt this mindset and methodology, especially if you want to have a growth mindset as a whole.

I thus urge all team members whether they come from HR, product development, operations, or any other department to come together and consider how we can ensure that we reach it and move closer to it.

Ideally, everyone contributes to the company's north star in some way. Particularly in terms of product development, we firmly believe that marketing can play a significant role from the very beginning.

When developing a product, using marketing and marketing tools can help you determine whether you're creating the right thing or if the features you're adding are actually required by the market.

You can utilize marketing to validate this, and when you successfully persuade the product team that you can offer them data and input about whatever they're producing, and give them feedback on whether or not there is a need for that in the market, it also becomes beneficial to them.

They can clearly understand that it's wonderful if you keep track of these things in the project or on the website because you can give us actual data that we can use for our next features or roadmap.

Therefore, strongly urge cooperation. If you have OKRs that are focused on growth marketing, it will benefit them, and it will be simpler to persuade the development team to support it if you also integrate the OKRs.

How would you assist a business that has a B2C product but is unsure of its target market?

Before spending any money on marketing if you are unsure of your target market, I would make a serious effort to spend time identifying your possible clients.

Using a tool that you are familiar with, such as Typeform or SurveyMonkey, create a survey or form.

Ask them to share it to as many people as they know by sending it to them. Additionally, gather useful information and make an effort to identify the initial target audience for your product.

A survey form could be quite useful in determining whether there is indeed a need. Additionally, it can be beneficial if you can chat to some individuals about your product and receive their comments.

Get the phase validation that I previously demonstrated in the innovation journey. So let's say you do an experiment with a budget, even if it is only $1,000. You design, let's say, one landing page or in that situation, perhaps even three to appeal to various target populations.

Then you let the ads run and observe which users respond better to those landing sites. Who is it then that is truly converting after clicking on your advertisement?

A different approach would be to develop a single landing page. I'll also give an example of a Facebook ad where a campaign can be created. Additionally, you have three distinct ad sets, each with a different target market.

Females in New York who are between the ages of 25 and 30 could thus be one of your target markets. A male living somewhere else could be the other target persona.

So you build up your queries or hypotheses about who your target audience could be as ad settings, and then you wait for the data to tell you who is responding to your advertisements, who is actually clicking on your landing page, who is converting, and who is contacting you.

That is one way to determine whether you are in an early stage. Even while we undertake marketing, I nonetheless constantly advise taking a step back before spending money on it, engaging with customers directly, and doing surveys. It should be so obvious, but we frequently choose not to do it because, you know, you always wonder who will fill it out.

However, we've consistently seen excellent results when creating surveys and dispersing them in large numbers, as well as when basically leaving our own bubbles and asking people to spread the word in order to get closer to your ideal customer.

You might even try testing in a B2B manner first before moving to B2C, if that's simpler. If you start with B2B, it doesn't follow that you can never switch to B2C.

I hope you liked this little growth marketing presentation. Along with learning about the most crucial tools, techniques, and abilities that support growth penetration, we went over the most crucial concepts and topics relevant to the subject.

* * *

Afterword

ABOUT THE AUTHOR

Samir Saif an Egyptian legal advisor and entrepreneur, I have played a key role in the establishment of many companies and startups in the fields of programming, technology, and business management. My expertise lies in seamlessly integrating the legal aspect with programming matters, making it easier for entrepreneurs to launch and grow their businesses. I am passionate about helping others succeed in the tech industry and look forward to facilitating the establishment of even more companies in the future.

Throughout my career, I have worked closely with a wide range of clients, from early-stage startups to established companies, to help them navigate the complex legal landscape of the tech industry. I have a deep understanding of the specific challenges and opportunities that come with starting and growing a tech-based business, and I use this knowledge to provide tailored, strategic advice to my clients.

In addition to my legal expertise, I am also well-versed in the latest trends and developments in the tech industry. This allows me to not only provide legal guidance, but also to identify potential opportunities and help my clients stay ahead of the curve.

As a successful entrepreneur myself, I understand the importance of taking a hands-on approach and working closely with my clients to help them achieve their goals. Whether it's incorporating a new business, negotiating contracts, or protecting intellectual property, I am dedicated to helping my clients succeed.

I believe that by combining my legal expertise with my understanding of the tech industry, I can play a crucial role in the success of the companies and startups I work with. And I look forward to continue to help them to achieve their goals and reach their potential in the future.

www.ingramcontent.com/pod-product-compliance
Lightning Source LLC
Chambersburg PA
CBHW050309220526
45465CB00005B/1918